Diana Helmerking

Fire Safety

Diana Helmerking

Fire Safety

BIRKHÄUSER

BASEL

Contents

Foreword

Ever since people adopted settled status, they constructed buildings to protect themselves from danger and the weather. However, in the case of unforeseen events like a lightning strike or fire, buildings themselves can easily present a danger to humans and animals. Providing adequate fire safety is therefore an important part of building design. This includes both preventive measures that can prevent fires from occurring, as well as measures that make it possible for people to be rescued from a building in the case of a fire and for the fire service to effectively contain the fire.

Fire safety involves more than meeting the requirements for safe building components and the design of escape routes, a major element in the layout of floor plans. Intelligent design solutions combine conceptual objectives, functional layout, and technology to create a comprehensive solution.

In order to be able to take these guiding ideas into account right from the beginning, it is necessary to be well informed about the requirements for fire safety and the options for achieving it. In addition to technical solutions, this involves an understanding of the causes and behavior of fire and the measures necessary to provide fire safety. It is important to understand fire safety issues as an integral part of the design process. To this end, *Basics Fire Safety* provides a comprehensive introduction enabling readers to carry out their own design work with a thorough understanding of the issues involved.

Bert Bielefeld, Editor

Introduction

Fire protection is a measure to avert danger. For the designer, fire protection measures appear to be relatively abstract because they deal, in theory, with cases of fire that hopefully will never occur. The idea of these measures is that when accidental fire and smoke occur, they do not spread and become a danger to humans, animals, the environment, or property.

When designing a building we deal with functional relationships: with the design of spaces and their use. Usually, we do not focus on technical and physical aspects until further down the line in the process. We need to consider, though, that fire protection issues play an important role in the design of floor plans, because fire compartments, escape routes, and stairwells have a strong impact on what is called zoning and on the formation of functional units. Therefore fire protection has to be an integral component of the design of buildings for every architect.

In this book the main focus is on fire protection aspects that need to be taken into account in the design work of architects and architectural students. This is not based on national regulations or the standards issued by the different States. Instead, various relationships are explained in order to promote a basic understanding of the issues involved in fire protection and to enable readers to apply the principles in their design processes.

Causes of fire

In order to understand the principles of preventive fire protection we need to first familiarize ourselves with fire and its causes.

FIRE

What causes fire?

A fire is the result of a combustion process. For combustion to take place, certain prerequisites for a fire must be in place at the same time. A combustible material (gas, liquid, or solid), together with oxygen from the air, forms an ignitable mixture. When the proportions of this mixture are favorable and an igniting energy is added, fire erupts. > Fig. 1 Whenever one of these components is missing, the danger of ignition no longer persists. > Fig. 2

Beneficial fire and destructive fire

A fire that remains in the place that has previously been chosen, for example in a stove or a place for a campfire, is a beneficial fire. However, if the fire leaves the previously chosen hearth or it occurs unintentionally, it becomes a destructive fire. Usually, destructive fires result in injury to people and/or damage to property or the environment. > Fig. 3 and Fig. 4

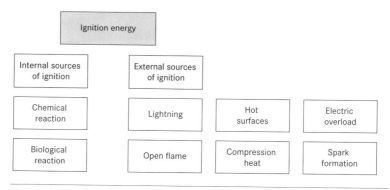

Fig. 1: Ignition energy

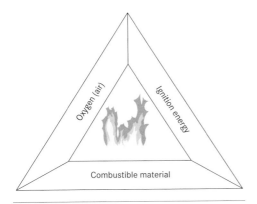

Fig. 2: Combustion triangle

Fig. 3: A bonfire is a beneficial fire

Fig. 4: Illustration of a large destructive fire

CATEGORIES OF FIRE

In order to be able to successfully plan and implement preventive fire protection measures, we need to be familiar with the causes of fire. These can be divided into different categories according to their type. > Tab. 1

Frequent causes of fire
Many fires are caused by faulty electric wiring, negligent everyday behavior, and human error. Fire insurance companies compile documents with overviews of the causes of fires based on the fire damage reported to them. > Fig. 5 It is possible to reduce the incidence of fires through education and preventive measures. > Chapter Avoidance of fire

Tab. 1: Causes of fire

Type of cause of fire	Example
Natural cause	Lightning
Caused by animals	Rodents biting into electric cables
Self-ignition without extraneous ignition energy	Cleaning rag saturated with oil
Technical cause	Defect in technical equipment
Negligence	Hot ash emptied into a combustible wastepaper bin
Arson (intentional)	Igniting the content of a trash can

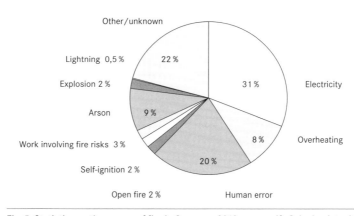

Fig. 5: Statistics on the causes of fire in Germany, 2018; source: Ifs Schadendatenbank

HOW FIRE DEVELOPS

A fire can be subdivided into different phases. In the first phase a combustible material is ignited and what develops is called an incipient fire; often, incipient fires can still be extinguished using a fire blanket or a hand-held fire extinguisher. The next phase is the development of the fire, which depends on the area on fire, the fire load, and the ventilation. If the flames spread and the temperature of the room air increases steadily, the destructive fire becomes a developed fire that requires the use of extinguishing equipment (sprinkler system, gas extinguishing system) or extinguishing apparatus used by the fire service. If the fire is not extinguished in this phase, it is possible for flashover to take place; when this happens, all combustible materials in the area on fire ignite and the fire spreads in a sudden burst. If it is not possible to extinguish the fire or the fire remains undetected, it becomes a fully developed fire, which is the next phase. > Fig. 6

In a fully developed fire the entire area on fire, including all objects, is burning, and the temperature can reach 1,000 °C and over. This leads to the fire spreading to adjoining spaces. If the fire is not detected at an early stage, the entire building will burn. <small>Fully developed fire</small>

When the temperature of the fire can no longer be maintained or increased because there are insufficient materials to burn or there is not enough oxygen reaching the fire, the fire will gradually die down. <small>Dying down of the fire</small>

When the oxygen content in a room is very low, an incipient fire cannot develop into a full fire. The temperature does not reach the ignition temperature. However, it can be high enough to trigger chemical processes of the materials in the room. In these processes, the heat leads to decomposition – also called pyrolysis. In this process, pyrolysis gases escape from the heated combustible materials, which in themselves are <small>Smoldering fire</small>

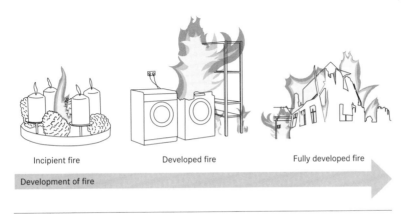

Incipient fire   Developed fire   Fully developed fire

Development of fire

Fig. 6: How fire develops

combustible but do not yet burn. The smoke from the fire of the incomplete combustion and the gases collect together in the layer of smoke, forming a toxic mixture. The components of the gas mixture depend on the materials; often the main component is carbon monoxide. This phase of the fire is called smoldering fire. Without additional oxygen, the fire cannot fully develop. If the room remains closed, the fire will die down due to a lack of oxygen.

Flashover The transition phase between the beginning of a fire in a closed room and the phase in which the fire reaches its maximum temperature is called flashover. This phase is characterized by a big increase in the temperature over a relatively short time. At the same time, the quantity of available oxygen in this room reduces due to the fire. The objects and surfaces in the room that have not yet caught fire continue to heat up due to the increasing temperature. When the temperature reaches ignition temperature and there is still sufficient oxygen available, the objects and surfaces will ignite even if there is no direct contact with flames. From that point onwards, all objects in the room that have reached ignition temperature will burn and the fire will become a fully developed fire.

Backdraft If, in the phase of a developing fire and increasing temperature there is not enough oxygen available, the heat may be sufficient to reach ignition temperature. Owing to the lack of sufficient oxygen, the objects, which at this point in time are not yet burning, will not yet start burning. However, if in this situation a large amount of oxygen is suddenly introduced to the room, for example when a door is opened or a window pane breaks, the smoke gas and the objects in the room ignite very rapidly and also start to burn. This process can be so rapid that it can lead to an explosion-like spread of the fire, a process called backdraft.

SMOKE

In the case of a fire, it is possible that the smoke and gases from the fire spread faster than the fire. Their composition and the danger they involve depend on the burning materials. In apartments there are many materials, most of which contain carbon. When these burn, this often leads to the development of dangerous smoke components and gases that have a toxic effect. When these are inhaled, they reach the organism via the lungs and cause changes to the lungs. As a result, it is harder to absorb and exchange oxygen and may not even be possible any more. This leads to smoke gas injuries, which reduce the chances of survival.
> Tab. 2

Soot Soot is not one of the fire gases and is produced primarily when combustion takes place rapidly and not enough oxygen can reach the fire. Because soot particles are very small (approx. 10 nm to 300 nm, that is, 1,000 times smaller than the diameter of a hair), they can be inhaled and thereby cause lung cancer.

Tab. 2: Fire gases

Gases	Properties	Fire load	Effects
HCl **Hydrogen chloride**	Can form hydrochloric acid in combination with water	Materials containing chlorine (PVC, pharmaceuticals, cooling agents)	Chemical burns to mucous membranes
HCN **Hydrocyanic acid**	Not stable, can decompose in an explosive process	Organic substances such as nylon, polyurethane (mattresses, upholstered furniture, carpets)	Deadly poison when inhaled
Dioxins (PCDD[1]/PCDF[2])	Highly poisonous	Substances containing chlorine	Damage to the skin and nervous system, disruption to hormonal balance and the enzyme systems
CO_2 **Carbon dioxide**	Displaces oxygen in the air	Organic substances (wood, leather, wool, fabrics)	Irritation of mucous membranes, shortness of breath (apnea), muscle cramps
CO **Carbon monoxide**	Is produced during combustion with insufficient oxygen; this gas is lighter than air	Inorganic substances (metals, plastic)	Sickness, headache; in high doses: loss of consciousness, apnea
SO_x **Sulfur oxides**	In combination with water can form sulfuric acid	Substances containing sulfur (coal, benzine, heating oil)	Chemical burns to mucous membranes
NO/NO_2 **Nitrogen oxides**	Poisonous	Products containing nitrogen	Damage to the respiratory tract

1 PCDD: Polychlorinated dibenzodioxins
2 PCDF: Polychlorinated dibenzofurans

Preventive fire protection

In fire protection a distinction is made between preventive and defensive fire protection. Preventive fire protection includes measures that prevent fires from occurring and from spreading, whereas defensive fire protection involves measures for rescuing people and animals, and for containing and fighting fire and smoke.

● The requirements for preventive fire protection involved in the construction or modification of a building are regulated to a large extent, with details included in regulations, standards, and guidelines.

However, underlying all these fire safety regulations are general principles, which are derived from technical and operative necessities. These general principles must be taken into account in the design of buildings, and are established and refined for the respective building project by the architects in cooperation with professional advisers and/or specialist fire safety engineers.

The design of buildings primarily focuses on aspects of preventive fire protection. > Fig. 7

The following subdivisions are made:

— Structural fire protection
— Plant-specific fire protection
— Organizational fire protection

Defensive fire protection

The tasks involved in defensive fire protection are primarily carried out by the fire service, who will try to rescue those at risk and extinguish the fire. > Chapter Defensive fire protection measures

> ● **Example**: In Germany, the key fire protection regulations are defined in the State Building Codes of the respective Federal States; in Great Britain they are embedded in the Building Regulations. As a rule, the respective provisions are further defined by technical instruments such as standards.

Fig. 7: Subdivision of fire protection

GENERAL PROTECTION OBJECTIVES

When a fire occurs, it is imperative to prevent damage to people, property, and the environment. The protection of the life and health of people and animals is the top priority, and is a general protection objective.

The general fire protection objectives for standard buildings (build- General objectives ings that are not of an unusual type and function) are defined in the statutory instruments of the respective States (e.g. in Germany, in the State Building Codes), and have the following principles in common: > Fig. 8

— Preventing the occurrence of fires and the spread of fire and smoke
— Rescuing people and animals
— Facilitating effective extinguishing work

In order to achieve the first protection objective, "Preventing fires Preventing fires from occurring and spreading and smoke from occurring and spreading", specific requirements are stipulated regarding the combustibility and fire resistance of building materials and components and the way in which spaces are enclosed. > Chapter Structural measures These measures are aimed at ensuring that rooms are structurally safe and free from smoke for a predefined period in order to make escape from the building possible. > Chapter Preventing the spread of fire

In the event of a fire, it must be possible to carry out rescue opera- Rescuing people and animals tions to ensure that people and animals can leave the endangered area or can be rescued from there. The first escape route, which must be provided in every building, allows for self-rescue, that is, rescue without help from a third party. The second escape route is a route that is available when the first escape route cannot be used. It provides an alternative escape option and is used by the fire service, after rescue operations have been completed, as a route of attack to fight the fire. This means that it must be secured for a certain period of time by adjacent building components that ensure its stability. > Chapter Design of escape routes Rescue activities and extinguishing by the fire service are considered to be part of defensive fire protection. > Chapter Making extinguishing possible

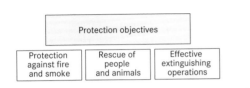

Fig. 8: General protection objectives

SPECIAL PROTECTION OBJECTIVES

Protection against
damage to property

Beyond the above, the objective is to prevent and limit damage from fire and smoke to property and the environment. These are considered special protection objectives and the respective protection measures include additional structural, organizational, and plant-specific measures. To minimize any residual risks, insurance companies and professional insurance associations have developed conditions and recommendations to ensure that – with the help of fast extinguishing action – commercial losses from operational and production interruptions are prevented. In view of the fact that insurance companies are interested in keeping damage to property due to fire to a minimum, they may stipulate additional measures as part of the insurance policies.

Part of the special protection objectives are also the preservation of building substance in the sense of the preservation of material assets or of historic building substance, the safeguarding of cultural heritage, and the maintenance of ongoing (State) operations (data safety, medical care, and military security).

● **Example:** Depending on the function of a building, there may also be further special protection objectives such as disaster prevention at a chemical factory, explosion protection for critical stock items, or the maintenance of certain functional areas, e.g. the OP section in a hospital.

Structural measures

Various measures can be taken to support structural fire protection. Firstly, the combustibility of building materials and furniture and fittings should be reduced as far as possible, and secondly, the spread of fire, smoke, and heat must be prevented by compartmentalization.

COMBUSTIBILITY OF BUILDING MATERIALS

The occurrence and development of a fire largely depends on the properties of the building materials. When these materials do not contribute to a fire due to their properties, the fire cannot spread to them. For this reason, building materials must comply with special requirements regarding their combustibility/flammability and are classified in accordance with their fire behavior; they are divided into different classes on the basis of standardized tests. There are international, European, national, and building regulation requirements. In a first step it is possible to distinguish between non-combustible and combustible building materials.

Non-combustible building materials consist primarily of substances that cannot be ignited. They may undergo change when exposed to heat, but in themselves do not constitute a fire risk or a fire load.

Combustible building materials are distinguished by the degree of their flammability/the extent to which they participate in the combustion process. They are therefore subdivided into easily inflammable, normally inflammable, and hardly inflammable building materials.

Building materials that are classified as easily inflammable (including once they have become part of the building or they have been processed) and building materials without stated performance characteristics (Germany DIN 4102: B3; Europe DIN EN 13501: F) are not permitted to be used in any new construction, conversion, or extension building. Easily inflammable building materials may only be used in construction in combination with other materials if all of the resulting material is no longer easily inflammable. > Tab. 3

Non-combustible building materials

Combustible building materials

●

● **Example**: Examples of combustible materials are wood, paper, wool, polystyrene, and straw. Non-combustible building materials include stone, clay, gravel, steel, brick, fired clay, glass, gypsum, and mortar.

Tab. 3: Fire behavior of building materials; European and German building material classes

Requirement	European classification DIN EN 13501	German classification DIN 4102
Non-combustible	A 1, A 2	A 1, A 2
Hardly inflammable	A 2, B, C	B 1
Normally inflammable	D, E	B 2
Easily inflammable	F	B 3

Tab. 4: Additional requirements relating to the classification of building materials as per EN 13501

Classification	Smoke development requirements (s = smoke)
s1	Low smoke development
s2	Medium smoke development
s3	High smoke development / smoke development not tested
Classification	**Burning droplets requirements (d = droplets)**
d0	No burning droplets / dropping material within 600 seconds
d1	No burning droplets / dropping material with a flame persistence of more than 10 seconds within 600 seconds
d2	No performance ascertained

Inflammability and smoke development

In addition to their inflammability, building materials are also tested for smoke development. The smoke development of building materials can obscure clear vision in an escape route, and the toxic components in smoke can have an effect on consciousness and health. When building materials are tested, it is also ascertained to what extent the respective building material forms burning droplets. The burning droplet of a plastic material can transfer the fire to another place and continue to spread. > Tab. 4

The fewer combustible building materials a building contains, the smaller its risk potential in the case of a fire. As a matter of principle, any building components used in the construction of escape routes must consist of non-combustible building materials.

FIRE RESISTANCE OF BUILDING COMPONENTS

When a fire breaks out, its spread should be prevented. To do this, any transfer routes are secured by separation so that fire, smoke, and heat cannot spread from one area or building to another.

Fire resistance time

Building components such as walls, floors, ceilings, and roofs must resist fire for a previously defined time to ensure that they prevent the spread of fire. The fire resistance of a building material specifies the necessary duration of functional integrity in minutes. Building materials are tested and assigned to fire resistance classes. Tab. 5 to Tab. 8 Loadbearing building components also must retain their loadbearing capability for a previously defined time when exposed to fire. Owing to their function/properties in the last phase of a fire, they are critical because the structural components of the building preserve its structural stability and thereby safeguard the escape routes.

Tab. 5: Fire resistance: building control terminology

Building control terminology	Fire resistance in minutes
Fire retardant	30 minutes
Highly fire retardant	60 minutes
Fire resistant	90 minutes
Highly fire resistant	120 minutes

Tab. 6: Building component requirements, European classification as per EN 13501

European designation		Building component requirement
R	Résistance (Resistance)	Loadbearing capability
E	Étanchéité (Sealing)	Integrity of space enclosure
I	Isolation	Thermal insulation when exposed to fire
M	Mechanical impact	Resistance to mechanical impact

Tab. 7: European classification of loadbearing building components

Building control requirements	Loadbearing component	
	With space enclosure	Without space enclosure
Fire retardant	REI 30	R 30
Highly fire retardant	REI 60	R 60
Fire resistant	REI 90	R 90
Firewall	REI 90-M	–

Tab. 8: European classification of non-loadbearing building components

Building control requirements	Non-loadbearing wall	
	Exterior	Interior
Fire retardant	E 30 (i > o) EI 30 (i < o)	EI 30
Highly fire retardant	E 60 (i > o) EI 60 (i < o)	EI 60
Fire resistance	E 90 (i > o) EI 90 (i < o)	EI 90
Firewall	–	EI 90-M

(i > o) from inside to outside   (i < o) from outside to inside

Classification of building components

In order to avoid unchecked spread of the fire, buildings are also divided into areas separated by fire-safety elements. These areas can consist of functional or residential units, stories, or fire compartments. The units are separated from each other by space-enclosing components, thus preventing spread of fire, smoke, and heat. The separation between these units consists of components that are at least fire retardant. In accordance with the European classification (DIN EN 13501), a check is carried out to establish for how long the space-enclosing components are retained and the transfer of heat during a defined fire is prevented for the protection of the neighboring unit. > Tab. 6

Reduction of heat radiation

Space-enclosing building components must be designed so that the temperature on the side away from the fire only rises to such a degree that, in this area, no ignition due to thermal radiation can occur. Heat radiation increases as the temperature rises and decreases in proportion to the distance. It is a form of heat transport.

Firewalls

The function of firewalls is to create and secure fire compartments. They must comply with strict requirements regarding fire resistance and structural integrity when exposed to fire and are built using non-combustible materials. Their dimensions must be sufficient not only to enclose the space, but also to resist mechanical impact (e.g. REI 90-M, EI 90-M).

Tab. 9: European classification of smoke protection as per EN 13501

European designation		Building component requirement
s	Smoke	 Impervious to smoke
c	Closing	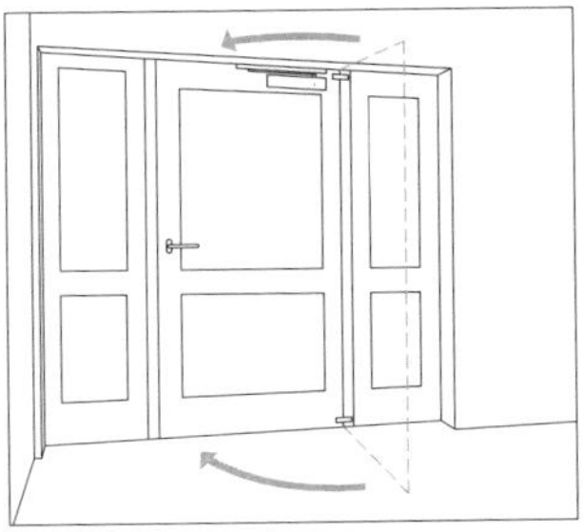 Self-closing

In order to ensure that smoke cannot spread unimpeded, the smoke permeability of the building components must be restricted. > Tab. 9 Openings in smoke and fire compartments must be reliably closed off with doors, shutters, or flaps.

Smoke protection

PREVENTING THE SPREAD OF FIRE

In addition to the building component requirements, physical separation must be provided in the design, such as an adequate distance between buildings or parts of buildings or physical compartmentalization within a building.

Building separation distances between neighboring buildings are distances that must be kept clear of structures in accordance with building code requirements. Their function is to provide a degree of privacy and to protect against the spread of fire. The idea of maintaining a defined distance between buildings is to prevent the fire of a burning building from spreading to a neighboring building. > Fig. 9

Building separation distances

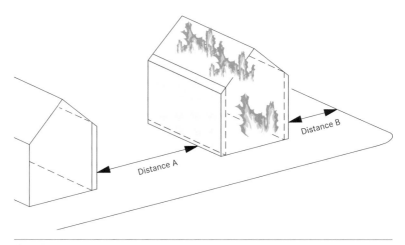

Fig. 9: External firewalls between the building and the boundary, and between buildings on the same plot

External compartmentalization

If it is not possible due to town planning provisions or the existing urban fabric to maintain adequate building separation distances, the building must be compartmentalized by providing firewalls to protect neighboring buildings. External firewalls must not have any openings such as doors or windows; as a rule, no openings are permitted. > Fig. 10

Internal compartmentalization

Internal firewalls are inserted when buildings are built in a row (e.g. semidetached houses, terrace houses) or within extensive buildings to create fire compartments. These firewalls are designed to prevent the spread of fire, smoke, and heat. Internal firewalls must extend to beneath the roof and, in the stories, should be placed above each other. Depending on the project, an offset arrangement may be permitted but is frequently subject to other conditions (compensatory measures). > Fig. 11

Spread of fire above the roof

When there is a fire in a row of attached buildings it is possible that the fire spreads above the roof. For this reason, measures must be included in the design that prevent the spread of fire to neighboring buildings. One of the possibilities is to extend the firewall that separates the buildings to above the roof. When the design includes a firewall that ends below the roof covering, additional fire-resistant slabs must be included at the level of the roof skin, consisting of non-combustible materials and projecting on both sides. > Fig. 12

Division into fire compartments

Firewalls are suitable means for subdividing extensive buildings to form fire compartments. The size/design of compartments is either determined by the permissible length (in Germany, maximum length of fire compartments is 40 m) or by separating functions (e.g. separating areas with a high fire risk from areas with no risk).

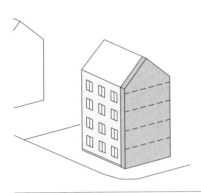

Fig. 10: External firewall

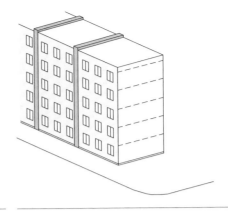

Fig. 11: Continuous internal firewall

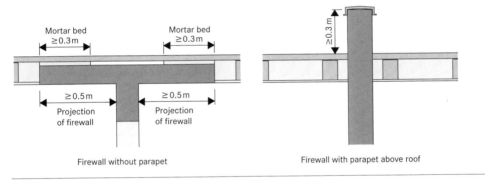

Fig. 12: Examples of detailing at the top of a firewall

Where buildings or parts of buildings are separated by a firewall but are laid out so that they meet in a corner, the firewall must be placed where it has a distance from the internal corner to ensure that the fire cannot spread from one part of the building across the firewall to the other part. > Fig. 13 and Fig. 14

Spread of fire in corners

○

○ **Note:** The German Model Building Code (MBO) Section 30 para. 6 stipulates a distance of 5 m. Where it is not possible to fulfill this requirement of the distance of the firewall from the internal corner, additional plant-related or structural measures must be provided to compensate for the shorter distance. > Chapter Compensation

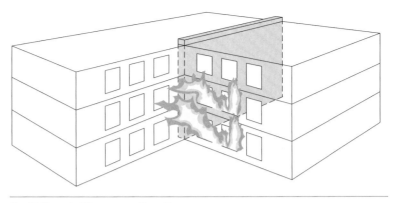

Fig. 13: Spread of fire across a firewall

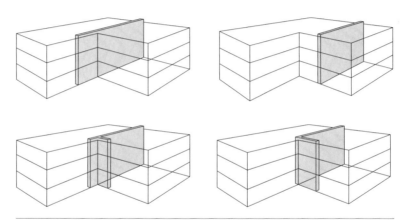

Fig. 14: Possible firewall arrangements

Vertical spread of
fire across building
components

When a fire spreads beyond the fire area, it may not only spread horizontally to adjoining rooms but also vertically via facades, stairwells, or ducts. In order to prevent vertical spread of fire it is possible, for example, that fire-resistant facade panels or projecting floor slabs are stipulated for facades.

Floor/ceiling slabs

Floor/ceiling slabs have a structural as well as a space-enclosing function and must be designed so that, in the case of a fire, they retain their structural properties for a defined period of time and resist the spread of fire. This also means that the fire must not be able to spread from below to above or from above to below through the floor. The connection of the floor/ceiling slabs to the facade must be designed so that the space-enclosing function can be fulfilled. The fire resistance requirements depend on the complexity of the building. Consequently, floor slabs above rooms with an increased risk of fire, such as those above workshops or laboratories, have to fulfill stricter requirements compared to those above a residential unit in which only a normal fire risk is to be expected. Separate considerations apply to the floor/ceiling slabs in basements and in attic stories.

Roofs must be protected against the impact of fire from the outside Roofs and the inside. Impact of fire from the outside can be in the form of flying sparks and/or radiant heat from a neighboring building and the roofing material must be resistant to these sources of fire. Roofs can be protected in this way with hard roofing materials that do not consist of combustible materials. > Fig. 15   ○

Where soft roofing materials are used larger distances are stipulated between the building and the boundary or neighboring buildings. Roofs must also be equipped to resist the spread of fire from the floor below in terms of fire resistance, resistance to the spread and transfer of fire, resistance to flying sparks, and radiant heat.

○ **Note**: Hard roofing materials may include stone slabs, roof tiles, slates, or roofing metals. Soft roofing materials such as reed or straw are less resistant to flying sparks and radiant heat.

F – Flying sparks/fire   R – Radiant heat

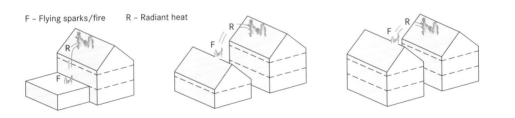

Fig. 15: Spread of fire

SMOKE COMPARTMENTALIZATION

In order to be able to limit the spread of smoke in the case of a fire it is necessary to form smoke compartments using walls and floors/ceilings and to adequately protect any openings such as doors or penetrations. >Chapter Smoke

Length of smoke sections

Without breathing apparatus, escaping an area filled with smoke to reach a safe area is possible only for about three minutes because of possible impairment of consciousness and poor vision. If a person cannot reach a safe area in that time (via a stairwell) and exit into the open, there is a risk that the person may become unconscious or die from asphyxiation. Likewise, for the purpose of the fire service, there should also be unobstructed vision after a certain distance to ensure that orientation in extensive buildings is possible. For this reason, the maximum length of a smoke section should be 30 meters. This can cover one or several stories. > Fig. 16

Height of smoke-free layer

In buildings with greater room heights (theaters, museums) the layer of smoke will not obscure vision and hence hamper escape quite so quickly, because for thermal reasons hot smoke will rise to the ceiling and the smoke-free space necessary for escape is maintained for longer. In such special buildings, there are technical devices (extinguishing systems, smoke and heat extraction systems) that can be used to ensure that a smoke-free layer is achieved for the time needed to escape. > Fig. 17 and > Chapter Smoke and heat extraction systems

Firestops in openings and penetrations

Neither fire nor smoke and heat must spread from the section with the fire to another section. In order to maintain the separating function of the building components, openings and penetrations should be reduced to a minimum. Openings in walls, floors/ceilings, and roofs are closed

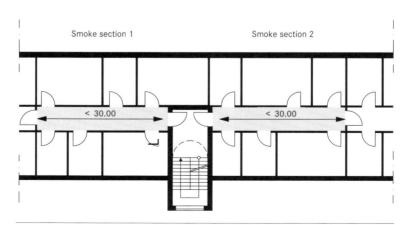

Fig. 16: Smoke sections

using fire- and smoke-stop devices, fire doors, or smoke protection doors. Likewise, penetrations for ventilation and other ducts, and for electric cables, are closed with suitable devices, for example, cable firestops or fire protection flaps. > Fig. 18

Fire doors of any size and fire protection flaps are suitable devices for securely closing openings or penetrations in fire-retardant or fire-resistant walls/firewalls in the case of a fire, and for providing the necessary compartmentalization. > Fig. 19 As a general principle, such firestop

Fire door

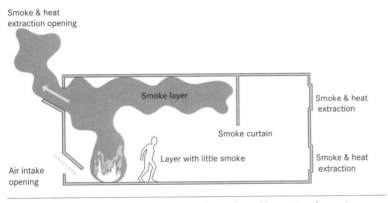

Fig. 17: Layer with little smoke due to the use of a smoke and heat extraction system

Fig. 18: Cable firestop

Fig. 19: Industrial-type fire door as fire protection closure

devices must be self-closing; they must engage in the lock of their own accord and must not be prevented from closing.

To ensure this, doors are fitted with overhead door closers or guide rail door closers. The overhead door closer is a special device that closes the door safely and automatically without any user action. Doors with guide rail door closers are fitted where free passage without prior door-opening action is required (barrier freedom). These doors have a holding function and are normally kept open. In the case of a fire, the closing action is triggered and the doors will close.

Smoke control doors

A smoke control door (smoke barrier) is a self-closing door that prevents the passage of smoke when closed. It is important to include this type of door in the design at the outset, because fire doors and smoke control doors can only be modified to a limited extent as a subsequent measure, as they may otherwise lose their approval as fire compartment components for the place where they are fitted.

Tight-fitting door

A tight-fitting door is a door that closes tightly and thereby provides a degree of fire compartmentalization. In some States tight-fitting doors are permitted as apartment entrance doors to protect the stairwell. These types of doors do not fulfill the full specification of fire or smoke control doors, but they are suitable for restricting the passage of fire and smoke for a short period of time (as a rule, less than 30 minutes) which, however, is not precisely defined. Tight-fitting doors have a permanently elastic seal on three sides, but no floor seal, and they are not self-closing.

O **Note**: When people try to escape from their apartment or office in the case of a fire, they do not remember to close the doors. This means, in the most unfavorable case, that the escape route fills with smoke and self-rescue is impossible. For this reason, it is not permitted to even temporarily prevent the closure of smoke protection doors and fire doors, e.g. by using wedges.

Plant technology

In order to also be able to meet all fire safety requirements in complex buildings or buildings with an increased risk of fire, plant-related measures are used in addition to structural measures. Where it is not possible to achieve the protection objectives with structural fire protection alone, the States can impose legislation, standards, guidelines, and conditions to ensure that people, and frequently also property, assets, and the environment, are protected in the case of a fire. These preventive and operative measures are referred to as plant-related fire protection. As a rule, a fire protection concept is produced to ensure that all structural, plant-related, and organizational measures optimally combine to fulfill the legal and insurance-related requirements.

WARNING SYSTEMS

Preventive measures such as the installation of a warning system make it possible to detect fires at an early stage and inform users without delay. A warning system can trigger a direct request for help and/or send an alarm message to the fire service, for example via an automatic transmission to the fire department.

A typical warning system is a fire alarm system, the function of which is to detect fires in the incipient phase, to warn the users of the building, to request help, to trigger fire protection systems, and to provide an overview to fire service operatives of where the fire was detected. The system has automatic fire alarms at relevant points/throughout the building, which detect a fire and send an appropriate message to the central fire alarm panel. It is possible to install fire alarms that identify a number of parameters (smoke, temperature, or flames) in order to respond appropriately to special functions. > Fig. 20 It is also possible to include non-automatic fire alarms (manual fire alarms) in such a system. The central fire alarm panel collects all information relating to detection or fire alarm

● Fire alarm system

● **Example**: In a listed building it is not possible to finish the walls of an escape route to REI 90 in accordance with the current regulations; it is only possible to reliably provide 30 minutes on the escape route. By installing a warning system it is possible to inform all users early enough for them to leave the building within 30 minutes, which means that the fire service does not have to search for people in the building.

faults. Depending on the event, the central fire alarm panel will trigger an automatic alarm and control various systems, for example, close the fire doors, switch off the air-conditioning system and sensitive equipment, or trigger an extinguishing system.

Fig. 20: Smoke alarm (automatic fire alarm, parameter: smoke)

Fig. 21: Fire alarms

○ **Note**: As a rule, alarms give out an acoustic and an optical signal in order to ensure that visually and hearing impaired people can be informed. This procedure is referred to as the two-sense principle. > Fig. 21

Fire service route maps

Fig. 22: Display panel, operating panel, and route map container for the fire service

Fig. 23: Manual fire alarm

It is possible to configure fire alarm systems so that a message is sent to the fire service in order to guarantee that the service is informed immediately (alarm transmission system with constant connection). The system will have a fire service panel for the fire service operatives, which is placed at the entrance of the fire service attack route. > Fig. 22 This provides an overview of where the system was triggered and/or which areas have reported a fire. The fire service panel is combined with route maps that show the fire service the way to the relevant alarm devices.
> Chapter Organizational and operational measures

In order to give people who are in the building the opportunity to report a fire manually, manual fire alarms are fitted at critical points in the building or in places with an increased fire risk. > Fig. 23

Manual fire alarms

SELF-HELP SYSTEMS

In order to make it possible for people to extinguish or fight an incipient fire, self-help systems are fitted in buildings. These self-help systems include manual fire extinguishers and wall hydrants.

Depending on the place where they are used, different types of fire extinguishers should be used with different extinguishing substances.

Manual fire extinguishers

●

● **Example:** Attempting to extinguish a grease fire in a kitchen with water will lead to a grease explosion. For this type of fire, special grease fire extinguishers are needed. Where fire extinguishers are fitted for the purpose of extinguishing fires on electrical or technical equipment, carbon dioxide fire extinguishers are needed because they do not leave any residue on the sensitive equipment.

In order to ensure that self-help devices such as manual fire extinguishers and wall hydrants > Figs. 24, 25 can be effectively used to fight incipient fires, people must be trained in the use of fire extinguishers as part of operational fire protection. > Chapter Organizational and operational measures

Fire extinguisher pictogram   Dry powder fire extinguisher   Carbon dioxide fire extinguisher

Fig. 24: Manual fire extinguishers

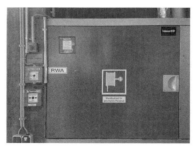
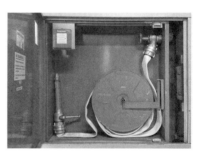

Closed   Open

Fig. 25: Wall hydrant

FIRE EXTINGUISHING SYSTEMS

Fire extinguishing systems are systems used for firefighting that are installed fixed and ready to operate, and that can be triggered both manually and automatically, for example via a fire alarm system. Depending on requirements, different types of fire extinguishing systems can be installed, for example, sprinkler systems, spray water systems, or gas, foam, or powder extinguishing systems. Fire extinguishing systems are devices for extinguishing a fire and preventing its spread. This reduces the danger to users, as well as damage to buildings.

A sprinkler system consists of a fixed installed network of water pipes and is used for fighting incipient fires. Sprinkler heads are part of the system and are connected to the network of water pipes. A glass ampoule fitted in the sprinkler head contains a special liquid with an air bubble. The liquid in the glass ampoule is temperature-sensitive and has a defined temperature at which it triggers; this depends on the size of the enclosed air bubble. In the case of a fire the temperature in the room increases, the special liquid becomes warmer and expands, the air bubble is compressed, and the glass ampoule shatters. This opens the nozzle of the sprinkler, and the extinguishing water starts to flow out from the water pipe network through the sprinkler in order to extinguish the fire. > Fig. 26 In the case of a fire, only those sprinklers where the respective trigger temperature is reached will be triggered; this is usually about 30 degrees above the permitted design temperature of the room.

Sprinkler system

If a fire extinguishing system is installed in a server or archive room, a sprinkler system would damage the servers or the archived items when the extinguishing system is triggered. In this case a gas extinguishing system is suitable, which would guarantee extinguishing action without water damage. In these systems, a gaseous extinguishing substance will be discharged from the outlets rather than water; this will replace the oxygen or affect the extinguishing action through a physical chemical process.

Gas extinguishing system

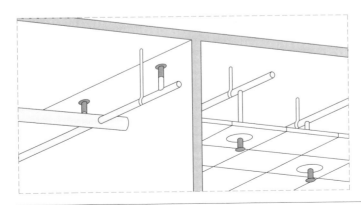

Fig. 26: Pipework of sprinkler system

SMOKE AND HEAT EXTRACTION SYSTEMS

In order to ensure that buildings or building sections are not completely filled with smoke, which would make escape and rescue difficult or impossible, smoke and heat extraction systems can be fitted. These systems control windows or openings in the roof or facades and open these so that the smoke can escape and layers with little smoke can be ensured. These systems can be triggered by hand switches or remotely.
> Fig. 27

The smoke can be extracted either by natural convection or by a fan.
> Fig. 28 In rooms with a height of up to 3 m natural smoke extraction cannot create a layer with little smoke due to the flow conditions. In this situation only the gases will escape through the openings, but the smoke will mostly remain in the room.

Fig. 27: Manual smoke extraction switch

Without smoke extraction

 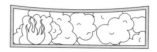 

With smoke extraction

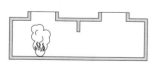 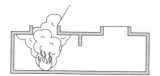 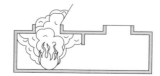

Fig. 28: Progress of fire in a building

Fig. 29: Smoke extraction fan

However, with the help of a pusher fan it is possible to remove smoke through the windows and discharge openings; these fans are placed by the fire service at the entrance to the functional unit, the smoke-filled room, or the entrance of the building. > Fig. 44 Mechanical smoke extraction relies on extraction fans to discharge the smoke. > Fig. 29 For this to work there must be smoke discharge openings and air replenishment openings of sufficient size in order to ensure that smoke, heat, and toxic fire gases can be discharged into the open air within a previously defined period.

EMERGENCY POWER AND LIGHTING

In order to ensure that the fire protection devices and other safety-relevant systems in the building are permanently available, an emergency power supply must be in place that can provide the necessary power to those systems in the building independent of the public electricity network. This can be provided by a diesel generator in the form of an independent electricity generator, by a battery system, or by an independent power supply. The electric installation needed for the distribution of the emergency power in the building must comply with fire safety standards in order to guarantee uninterrupted operation.

Emergency power supply

In the case of failure of the power supply, emergency lighting provides general artificial lighting also where visibility is poor (darkness, obscuration through smoke, or power failure). In the case of danger, emergency lighting helps orientation and makes it easier to find and use rescue routes.

Emergency lighting

Fig. 30: Rescue route pictograms

Rescue signage

Rescue signage consists of rescue route pictograms. > Fig. 30 To ensure that these signs can be seen in an emergency, they must have the benefit of emergency lighting which, in the case of a power failure, is operated by a battery or an emergency power supply.

An alternative to signs that do not rely on power are photoluminescent rescue pictograms, which indicate the route to an emergency exit for a short period via stored fluorescent light. However, these signs are only permitted in areas with low complexity because of their limited effect.

COMPENSATION MEASURES

Deviation from standard solutions

Often there are situations in which adequate fire protection cannot be exclusively achieved via structural measures. This may be due to various reasons, for example:

— A multistory atrium is to contain open staircases and lifts, as well as areas where people linger, and at the same time is to be used as an escape route.
— The subdivision of a production building into smaller fire compartments is not possible due to the large scale of the production plant.
— Explosive and poisonous substances are used in a laboratory building; these substances must not be allowed to reach the environment in the case of a fire.
— A high-bay storage building contains a large amount of combustible material.
— An assembly hall is designed for 600 people who, in the event of a fire, have to leave the hall without risk.
— In a listed building existing walls and doors cannot be replaced or upgraded to meet current requirements.
— In an existing building the length of the escape route between two stairwells is a bit longer than currently stipulated in the regulations.

When, in such cases, it is not possible to comply with the relevant Compensation requirements for preventive fire protection, compensatory fire measures must be used so that the protection objectives can be achieved in a different way. The respective protection objective describes why something should be achieved; this is translated into a law governing the distance, for example the maximum length of a fire compartment of 40 meters. Where plant-related fire protection measures are used, such as a fire alarm system or a sprinkler system throughout the building, larger fire compartments in buildings of a special type and function can be permitted. Such plant-related systems can be used to compensate for an inadequate situation. Early automatic detection of incipient fires and firefighting with the help of automatic extinguishing systems mean that the loads supported by the loadbearing structure of the building as a result of fire are reduced, and also that there will be less smoke. This makes it possible to successfully negotiate a longer rescue route distance to reach the next safe section.

In summary, compensation measures are usually those measures that provide earlier information to those at risk or to the rescuers, or make it possible to directly fight or control an incipient fire. In view of the fact that deviations from the stipulated standards are always subject to individual approval, compensation measures have to be designed in each individual project and have to be agreed upon by the authorities and the fire service. > Fig. 31

● **Example**: In accordance with statutory provisions, the floors in office buildings functioning as horizontal closures or fire compartments must comply with REI 30 or REI 90 as a preventive measure against the spread of fire and smoke. This would preclude an office building being designed as an atrium building. To make an atrium design possible, it is therefore necessary to apply for a deviation from the requirement for continuous floors. As compensation the design includes an automatic extinguishing system, an early fire detection system using fire alarms, and a mechanical extraction system for the atrium. In order to ensure that smoke cannot be drawn into other stories owing to the open connection, additional smoke curtains are designed that will close the opening to the atrium in the case of smoke occurring. > Fig. 32 This means that all users and the fire service are immediately informed in the case of a fire, that the fire is controlled through automatic extinguishing devices, and that the escape routes are kept free of smoke. Evidence of whether the planned compensation is adequate is often provided using engineering calculation methods.

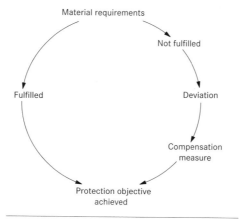

Fig. 31: Compensation

Fig. 32: Protecting an entrance hall with smoke curtains

Design of rescue routes

Should a fire break out in a building, it must be possible for all people and animals to reach safety and open air via reliable routes. The protection objective "Rescuing people and animals" has top priority. For this scenario, escape and rescue routes are provided in the building that make it possible to leave the building independently and safely. These routes consist of circulation routes (passageways, corridors, staircases) that comply with special requirements (size, length, finish), which firstly make escape possible (escape route) and secondly allow the fire service operatives to carry out rescue operations (rescue route).

BUILDING TYPES AND FUNCTIONS

The requirements for and the design of the rescue routes depend on the type and function of the building. One of the aspects to take into consideration is the fire risk associated with a certain function, and how many people have to be rescued or have to be able to escape in the case of a fire. If there is no risk or only a very small risk, the fire protection requirements will be minimal. The requirements for fire protection become stricter as the number of functional units and users, and the height of the building, increase. However, buildings of a special type and function such as a hospital, a high-rise building, a laboratory building, or school are subject to strict requirements regarding preventive fire protection. These buildings are special buildings with special requirements regarding structural, plant-related, and organizational fire protection, which are frequently defined in specific guidelines or regulations (e.g. Industrial Building Directive, Model Ordinance Governing Places of Assembly).

●
Fire risk

The use of fire protection measures increases as the fire risk increases. In the case of special buildings this is subdivided into low, medium, and high. > Tab. 10

● **Example**: In Great Britain, buildings are divided into dwelling houses, large dwelling houses up to 3 floors, large dwelling houses over 3 floors, and buildings not used for residential purposes (defined in Approved Document B). Then there is the group of special buildings, which is subdivided into risk classes (defined in British Standard 9999). Buildings in China are also divided according to height, type of building, and function. A distinction is made between civil buildings (residential buildings up to 27 m, 27 m to 54 m, and taller than 54 m), public buildings (up to 24 m, 24 m to 50 m, and taller than 50 m), and finally, factories and warehouses. The fire protection requirements for these buildings are subdivided into four classes (I, II, III, IV) (Fire Protection Standard GB 50016-2014).

Examples	Low	Medium	High
Administration, services	Offices without file storage	Offices with file storage	Theater stages
Industry	Concrete factory	Bread factory	Furniture production
Trade, retail	Sales rooms with non-combustible items	Sales rooms with combustible items	Stores with paints or cleaning agents

Standard buildings   Buildings without/with low fire risk below the high-rise building limit are classed as standard buildings; these include, for example, housing, office, and administration buildings. The high-rise building limit is defined by the height at which it is no longer possible to provide a second rescue route via aerial rescue trucks (ladder trucks). > Fig. 33

It is necessary, at the design stage, to establish what rescue equipment the fire service has at its disposal for the respective building in order to be able to clarify the maximum height for a second rescue route involving rescue equipment. Should the necessary equipment not be available, alternatives must be considered, for example a second rescue route within the building or a suitable external staircase. > Fig. 47

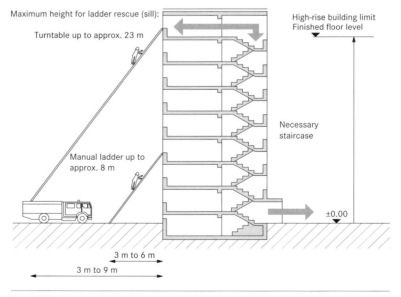

Maximum height for ladder rescue (sill):

Turntable up to approx. 23 m

High-rise building limit
Finished floor level

Manual ladder up to approx. 8 m

Necessary staircase

±0.00

3 m to 6 m

3 m to 9 m

Fig. 33: First and second rescue routes, options for rescue ladders

Buildings are referred to as special buildings when it is deemed that they have a greater fire risk due to their type and function. > Tab. 11 For this reason, they are subject to special requirements regarding structural, plant-related, and organizational fire protection. Frequently, additional statutory regulations apply because the requirements are stricter than those for standard buildings. Special buildings require at least two structural rescue routes because, owing to their height (high-rise buildings) or their large number of visitors (sports stadiums, shopping centers), an alternative escape and rescue route can only be provided by structural means. The objective is to design the escape and rescue routes so that self-rescue is possible and, in the best possible case, is already complete when the fire service reaches the building. This means that the fire service can immediately start extinguishing operations. If it is a building with people who are dependent on help, for example, babies and small children in a day nursery, sick or elderly people in a hospital, elderly residents in sheltered accommodation, or people with disabilities, additional organizational measures have to be planned at an early stage in order to

Special buildings

Tab. 11: Characteristics of special buildings

Characteristics of special buildings:	Examples
Buildings where, owing to their height, ladders cannot be used as rescue routes	High-rise buildings
Buildings where large numbers of people congregate	Stadiums, theaters, trade fair buildings
Buildings for people who depend on help from others	Day nurseries, hospitals, care homes
Buildings frequented by day visitors without knowledge of the premises	Museums
Buildings where people without knowledge of the premises stay overnight	Guesthouses, hostels, hotels
The type and function of the building makes it necessary to include large functional units	Industrial buildings, trade fair halls

ensure that these groups also can safely escape to the open. > Chapter
Organizational measures, Figs. 53–54

Habitable rooms

The length of a rescue route is measured from the habitable room that is furthest away from the nearest exit to safety. Rooms are referred to as habitable rooms when they are suitable and designed for people to remain in them for longer periods. In apartments, typical habitable rooms are the lounge, kitchen, dining room, and bedrooms. Bathrooms, restrooms, storerooms, and corridors are not habitable rooms because as a rule people do not spend extended periods in them. > Tab. 12

Functional units

Rooms may either be part of a functional or a residential unit. Rescue routes in buildings are always routes that lead out of a functional or a residential unit. Sections defined as functional units can vary a great

Tab. 12: Allocation of rooms

Habitable room	Non-habitable room
Bedroom	Walk-in closet
Nursery	Restroom/WC
Kitchen	Bathroom
Dining room	Corridor
Lounge	Storeroom
Office	Plant room
Workshop	Kitchenette
Professional practice premises	Washroom
Seminar room	
Shop	

○ **Note:** In hospitals, elevators for the evacuation of patients in beds have to be included in the design, in addition to two structural rescue routes. In the necessary stairwells, zones for wheelchair users and/or beds on wheels have to be provided in the design, which must be arranged so that the respective equipment does not obstruct the escape route. From these safe areas, people can be collected one by one by members of staff or care personnel and taken into the open (evacuation). Elevators, the use of which as a means of rescue is guaranteed in the case of a fire, can be used to help with the rescue of these people with restricted mobility. If a whole ward has to be evacuated in a hospital, it must be possible to push patients in beds safely to a neighboring ward. > Chapter Types of rescue routes deal in their function (e.g. offices, workshops, shops, apartments) and require a rescue route system with two rescue routes. This makes it possible for people to escape into the open or into a secure area from every functional unit, independent of any other units. A design with just one rescue route is only sufficient for functional units without habitable rooms.

The number of functional units and their respective size are also important for the risk assessment. A building with many functional units would be subject to stricter requirements regarding preventive fire protection because, in the event of a fire, the rescuers will have to secure more sections.

Number of functional units

The functional units must be separated from each other in terms of fire safety using space-enclosing and fire-resistant components (walls, floors, roofs) in order to ensure that fire, smoke, and heat cannot pass directly from one functional unit to another. > Chapter Preventing the spread of fire

Enclosure principle

Between functional units and also for the compartmentalization of rooms with an increased fire risk compared to rooms with a lower fire risk (laboratories/normal office use), the minimum requirement is fire-retarding separating walls. In this way it is possible to create fire resistance and contain a fire for a defined period of time, sufficient for people to escape to a safe area. Openings in these walls must be limited to a minimum and must be secured with fire-retarding, leak-proof, and self-closing closures. An element that encloses a room, such as a separating wall, needs to extend up to the floor above or any other horizontal closure at the top or the roof covering. > Fig. 34

Separation of functional units

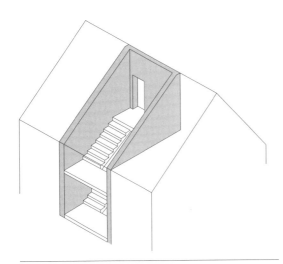

Fig. 34: Separating wall up to the level of the roofing material

TYPES OF RESCUE ROUTES

As a general principle, two rescue routes must be available that are independent of each other. If one escape and rescue route cannot be used, there is then an alternative option available for escape.

First rescue route The first rescue route must lead to the open or a safe area over the shortest possible distance and must have an exit directly at ground level. This applies both to a single-story freestanding single-family dwelling and to a multistory building. The first rescue route is a structural escape and rescue route, which can be used without third-party help and makes it possible to leave the building safely. In the case of a fire it provides a safe route for rescuers to help animals and people who cannot escape by themselves (those needing help) and, thereafter, is a route of attack for carrying out extinguishing operations. This means that a fire inside a building can be controlled and hopefully also extinguished. For this reason the structural integrity of the rescue route must be guaranteed for a defined period of time to ensure that the rescuers are not at risk.

Second rescue route Buildings with habitable rooms must have at least two rescue routes that are independent of each other. The second rescue route may be a route via the fire service's rescue equipment (portable ladder, turntable ladder) or a second structural rescue route. > Fig. 35 Owing to the complexity of the building, that is, its height, the number of users, its accessibility, or considerations regarding the difficulty of rescuing people, a second structural rescue route may be stipulated.

Safe stairwell When a building has the benefit of a safe stairwell it may be possible to omit a second rescue route. The safe stairwell is a special necessary stairwell. > Chapter Necessary stairwell Such a stairwell is designed so that its structure and/or technical equipment prevents fire and smoke from entering it, and is therefore available for escape and rescue at all times.
> Fig. 46

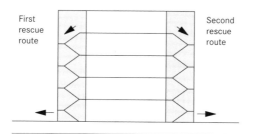

Fig. 35: Two structural rescue routes

In high buildings and in buildings with people who cannot rescue themselves via staircases (e.g. hospitals), a safety, evacuation, or fire service elevator is provided as an additional measure. The structure and/ or technical equipment of this must be designed so that the elevator can also be safely used in the case of a fire (safety and functionality in the case of fire). It can be combined with a safe stairwell.

Elevators as a means of rescue

RESCUE ROUTE REQUIREMENTS

One of the most important design tasks in every building is to provide a first rescue route from the stories to the open. The design of first rescue routes is subject to some general requirements:

General requirements for a first rescue route

— Escape and rescue routes must be as short as possible and sufficiently wide.
— The doors out of a necessary corridor or stairwell, as well as all subsequent doors, must open in the direction of escape. The first door from a habitable room to a necessary corridor may open in either direction.
— Doors along escape routes must not reduce the specified width of the escape route (e.g. on the landings of stairwells). The stipulated escape route width must be provided throughout the entire escape route to the open, without any bottlenecks.
— The end points must have exits directly at ground level or into a safe area.
— Depending on the period of time needed for maintaining the function, the building components enclosing necessary corridors and stairwells must be designed to meet the respective fire protection objective.
— Rescue routes must not contain any fire loads or obstacles and must be compartments that are separate from other parts of the building.
— Any ducts, channels, or openings along the rescue route must be reduced to the minimum necessary and must be secured.

Owing to the position, use, and size of the building, the different sections of a rescue route have to comply with different requirements to ensure that all users of the building can leave it as quickly as possible in the case of a fire. These are specified in laws, directives, guidelines, and technical rules. In addition, investors, insurance companies, or listed building departments stipulate further measures.

Such provisions may be in the following areas:

— The maximum length of rescue routes (e.g. in Germany, 35 m)
— The design of necessary corridors
— The design of necessary staircases

- The design of necessary stairwells/safe external staircases
- The design of safety stairwells
- The design of exits to the open
- How to deal with installations on rescue routes
- The size and arrangement of windows that are used as rescue routes

Length of rescue routes In the event of a fire it must be possible to reach the open via a previously defined length of route. The different lengths of rescue routes and measuring methods are defined in the laws, directives, and guidelines of the States. > Tab. 13 They depend on the type of building, the degree of risk, and what plant-related devices are used. > Chapter Plant-related measures

Single-family dwelling requirements The requirements for rescue routes become stricter as the complexity of a building increases. In a freestanding single-family dwelling there are no particular fire protection requirements because it is assumed that the fire risk is low and that the inhabitants are familiar with the place. Should the inhabitants discover a fire and smoke or receive a fire warning via a smoke detector, they make their way to safety via the normal corridor or stairwell. The corridor and stairwell are not subject to special requirements regarding fire protection; they lie within the residential unit. This first rescue route allows the inhabitants to reach the open directly via the front door or another external door. The routes are short and the inhabitants are familiar with them. Once they have reached safety in the open, the fire service can start extinguishing operations. > Chapter Fire service tasks If inhabitants remain in the dwelling, they can be rescued by the fire service.

Rescue window as second escape route If there is only one structural escape route, it must be possible for inhabitants at risk in an upper floor to reach the fire service ladder via a window, which means that only windows with an adequate width and height are suitable.

Tab. 13: Examples of permitted rescue route lengths

Act/Directive	First rescue route: Reachable from at least one exit to the open or a necessary stairwell	Meters (max.)
Standard building (BauO NRW)	From any place in a habitable room to the stairwell or the open	35 m
Places of congregation (SBauVO NRW)	From any visitor seat to the nearest exit from the place of congregation (not longer than 30 m)	30 m
High-rise buildings (SBauVO NRW)	From any place in a habitable room and in a basement floor	35 m
Sales premises (SBauVO NRW)	From any place in a sales room	25 m
Workplace (Workplace regulations)	From rooms with an increased fire risk without automatic fire-extinguishing systems	25 m
BauO NRW Building Code, North Rhine-Westphalia	SBauVO Special Building Regulations, North Rhine-Westphalia	

Buildings with many functional units and extending through several stories that are higher than can be reached with portable ladders, that is, about 7 m above ground level to the finished floor level, are more complex than single-family dwellings. In such buildings, a larger number of people (inhabitants, employees, visitors) from various sections (stories, residential units, functional units) are expected to try to escape in the case of a fire. Therefore these buildings are subject to stricter requirements regarding preventive fire protection. These buildings must have a necessary stairwell and, depending on the number of functional units, a necessary corridor. In many cases, a second structural rescue route is also obligatory.

RESCUE ROUTE SECTIONS

Rescue routes can be divided into horizontal and vertical sections. A standard first rescue route leads from a habitable room into the necessary corridor and on to the open via a necessary stairwell with a necessary staircase. > Fig. 36 In complex buildings the second rescue routes are subject to the same design requirements. In simple buildings there are alternative options. > Chapter Additional forms of second rescue routes

Escape routes are measured beginning from the furthest habitable room, including a notional route through that room, to the exit of the residential or functional unit. > Fig. 36 That notional route together with the necessary corridor makes up the horizontal part of the rescue route. If the room is at ground level, the route leads via the necessary corridor to the open or directly from the room to the open.

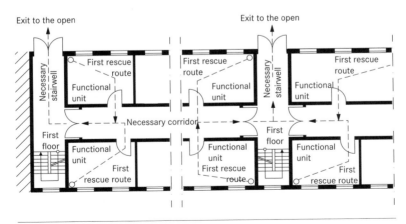

Fig. 36: Sections of a rescue route: from the functional unit to the open

Necessary corridor A necessary corridor links the respective residential or functional unit with the necessary stairwell. A second rescue route must be available as an alternative escape option. Horizontal rescue routes do not have to be independent of each other and, within the story, can lead via the same necessary corridor. > Chapter Necessary corridor

Vertical rescue route The first vertical rescue route runs via a necessary staircase. Vertical rescue routes provide access from and to the exits of functional units or necessary corridors. > Fig. 37 All functional units that are not at ground level must have access to two vertical rescue routes. These must be independent of each other and preferably be arranged in opposite directions. The second rescue route can be via the fire service's rescue equipment, a safe external staircase, or another necessary staircase within a necessary stairwell. Should it not be possible to provide more than one rescue route in a building, there is the option of providing the vertical part of the rescue route via a safe stairwell. > Chapter Necessary stairwell

Exit to the open At the end of the necessary stairwell is the exit to the open. This is the last section of a rescue route and may lead directly or indirectly to the open. Usually, an exit door leads directly to the open. If the stairwell is somewhat distant from the outside, the rescue route must be continued via a passageway that meets the same fire protection requirements as the stairwell and must then lead to the open. From there, it should be possible to reach a public area where escaped people can be taken care of and taken to safety.

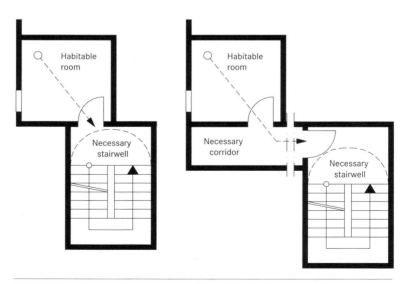

Fig. 37: Options for accessing a necessary stairwell (vertical rescue route)

NECESSARY CORRIDORS

Necessary corridors are used as escape and rescue routes by a number of different functional units or residential units and therefore must meet stricter requirements regarding freedom from fire and smoke.

Width of a necessary corridor

In order to ensure that safe escape via the necessary corridor is possible in the case of a fire, the minimum width of rescue routes is determined in accordance with the largest number of people that have to use the escape route in an emergency. The calculation is carried out on the basis of the size of the functional units.

Once the width of the escape route has been calculated, this must be included in the design of the necessary corridors and the onward rescue route system. As a rule, the necessary corridor in a residential or office building should not be less than 1 m wide, and in public buildings, not less than between 1.20 and 1.50 m. However, frequently necessary corridors have to be significantly wider than the necessary clear width, for example when doors open on to the corridor or when intermediate doors reduce the clear width due to the thickness of their frames. > Fig. 38   ○

● **Example:** If a necessary corridor serves 5 functional units with an average of 20 people each, the corridor must be wide enough to allow 100 people to escape safely. If a necessary corridor serves 5 residential units with not more than 4 people each, the clear width of the corridor must not be wider than is necessary for 20 people to escape safely. In special buildings, it is often necessary to allow for a large number of people, such as a theater with 1,000 seats or a stadium with 20,000 seats.

○ **Note:** In Germany, the width of the escape routes from workplaces is specified in the "Technical Rules for Workplaces, Escape Routes and Emergency Exits, Escape and Rescue Plan". > Tab. 14

Tab. 14: Width of escape routes from workplaces (ASR A2.3)

Number of people (catchment area)	Clear width (in m)
Up to 5	0.875
Up to 20	1.00
Up to 200	1.20
Up to 300	1.80
Up to 400	2.40

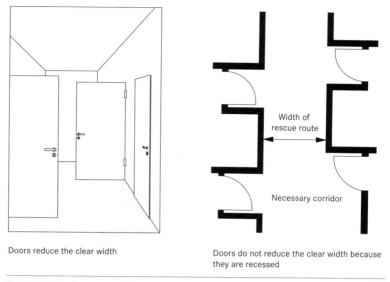

Doors reduce the clear width

Doors do not reduce the clear width because they are recessed

Fig. 38: Width of rescue route in a necessary corridor

Width of rescue route

Necessary corridor

Smoke section

Longer necessary corridors have to be subdivided into smoke sections using smoke barriers after a maximum of 30 m. Should a fire event lead to part of a necessary corridor being filled with smoke, escaping people can reach a safe area within a distance of not more than 30 m.
○ > Fig. 16

The required barriers that form the smoke section must be designed so that they prevent the passage of smoke (smoke-tight) and are self-closing in order to prevent the passage of smoke to the adjoining area for a specified time (approx. 10 minutes). In order to ensure that all sections of the escape route are available at all times, it must not be possible to lock smoke control doors. > Chapter Smoke compartments

Requirement for enclosing building components

The walls of necessary corridors are space-enclosing components and must be at least "fire-retarding"; the materials used for plaster, insulation, linings, etc. must be "non-combustible". The required fire resistance is determined in accordance with the need to maintain the

○ **Note:** When areas are filled with smoke, the reason is often because doors from residential units that have caught fire are not closed by escaping people or because self-closing doors are kept open using wedges or similar devices – something that is not permitted.

necessary function as an escape and rescue route and, possibly, as a route of attack for the fire service. A necessary corridor should not contain any additional furniture or technical equipment in order to avoid additional fire loads. Furthermore, any tripping hazards should be avoided; a difference in height in a necessary corridor must not have more than three steps. Doors that lead to this part of the horizontal rescue route must not open in a way that reduces the clear width of the necessary corridor or even represent obstacles to escaping people. > Fig. 39 Doors and other closing devices should be smoke-tight and self-closing. In residential units it may, in certain cases, be adequate to select tight-fitting doors.

Other openings in necessary corridors should be limited to what is absolutely necessary. Internal windows in the form of fixed clerestory windows should be placed above the heads of any escaping people (> 1.80 m). The glass must have a minimum resistance to fire and combustion gas. > Fig. 40 If glazing is intended at a lower level, it is level with the escape route and must therefore be capable of preventing heat radiation in the direction of the necessary corridor with the help of classified fire-protection glazing. > Fig. 41

Glazing in a necessary corridor

Fig. 39: Furniture representing tripping hazards and fire loads in a necessary corridor

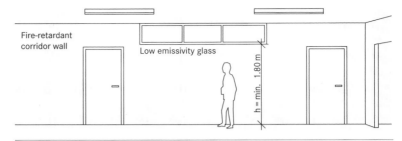

Fire-retardant corridor wall

Low emissivity glass

h = min. 1.80 m

Fig. 40: Necessary corridor with low emissivity glass

Fire-retardant corridor wall

EI fire-resistant glazing

Fig. 41: Necessary corridor with EI fire-resistant glazing

Technical installations

Where it is unavoidable to install pipework or cables along a necessary corridor, these must be secured with classified building components as they represent fire loads. Suitable devices are firestops for cables and pipes, and also fire protection flaps. > Chapter Preventing the spread of fire

"Captive" rooms

Captive rooms are considered special cases for the purpose of horizontal rescue routes. For such habitable rooms that are located behind or next to another room and can only be entered or left via that other room, additional measures are necessary to make the escape route safe. A captive room may be given access to a first rescue route by installing a second exit or it may be fitted with a sightline through to the preceding room. This would mean that a person in that room can detect any danger, and people in that captive room can be warned. Alternatively, it is possible to fit a horn or siren in the captive room that will be triggered by a fire alarm system. > Fig. 42 and Chapter Warning systems

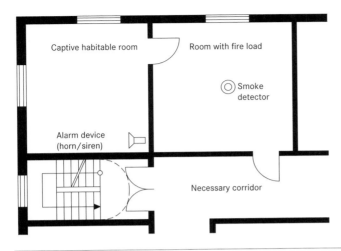

Fig. 42: Captive room with connection to a fire alarm system

NECESSARY STAIRWELLS

As with a necessary corridor, necessary stairwells and necessary staircases are subject to specific requirements. A stairwell is a safe area and part of a rescue route and as such must be safe from fire, smoke, and heat long enough to enable people and animals to escape from the building and to allow the fire service to carry out rescue operations via the vertical rescue route.

In order to facilitate swift escape, a necessary stairwell must be continuous and should not be continued at different places in the different stories. The width should be designed to suit the number of people expected; this number must take into account those escaping from several necessary corridors, in which case it may be necessary to design wider staircases.

Staircase geometry

∎

∎ **Tip:** A necessary staircase should be at least 1 m wide to facilitate safe escape. Within a residential unit this can be reduced to 0.80 m. In special buildings the clear width should not be less than 1.20 to 1.50 m, thus providing space for several people side by side.

When designing landings it is important to ensure that doors opening from necessary corridors into the stairwell do not restrict the required clear width of the movement area in the vertical escape route. At the top landing the first step must not be immediately behind a door, since this could represent a fall hazard. Handrails must be fitted firmly and securely; in wider stairwells and public buildings handrails must be fitted on both sides, thus curtailing the clear width of the escape route.

Requirement for adjoining building components

A necessary stairwell is formed with space-enclosing building components that are at least fire retardant. The fire resistance class of enclosing building components depends on the size and function of the building and the number of functional units. This also applies to the building materials, which must consist of non-combustible materials as a minimum requirement. Any openings in the stairwell must be closed off tightly and must be self-closing.

Lighting in the necessary stairwell

To make it possible to reach the exit safely, necessary stairwells must be lit by natural or artificial means. Depending on the height of the building, and in special buildings, safety lighting may be stipulated.

Protection from smoke

To ensure that smoke from a functional unit cannot pass into the vertical rescue route, the exits from the functional units should have self-closing doors provided there is no preceding anteroom or necessary corridor between the door and the stairwell. In addition, a facility must be available to ensure that any smoke that has entered does not impede the escaping people. If the stairwell is located on the inside of an external wall, the smoke can be discharged via suitable openable windows on the floors above ground level provided air can be replenished from an opening at ground level (e.g. the exit to the open). > Fig. 43 This can be mechanically enhanced by the fire service with the help of a pusher fan. > Fig. 44

Internal stairwell

If it is not possible to ventilate to the outside via windows (fixed glazing or internal stairwell), an opening for the discharge of smoke has to be fitted at the topmost place in the stairwell; operation of this must be possible from first floor and top floor levels. > Fig. 45 In some cases it may

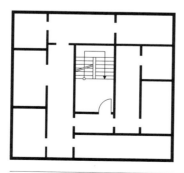 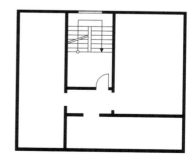

Fig. 43: Position of stairwell

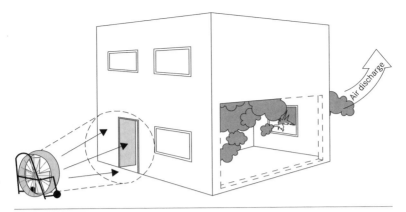

Fig. 44: Pusher fan in front of the entrance door

also be necessary to install an automatic smoke extraction system. > Chapter Smoke and heat extraction systems

Safety stairwells are specially designed stairwells. They are designed so that neither fire nor smoke can enter the stairwell. This means that they are permanently free from smoke. The design of safety stairwells can be based on structural or plant-related arrangements. > Fig. 46 In the case of a structural safety stairwell, the route from a necessary corridor leads to an open passageway that is exposed to the open flow of wind so that the smoke from a fire can be blown away and does not enter the

Safety stairwells

Fig. 45: Smoke discharge from the stairwell

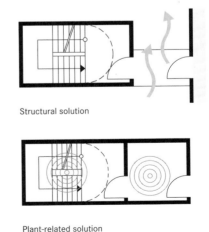

Structural solution

Plant-related solution

Fig. 46: Safety stairwell

stairwell. The passageway connects the building with the safety stairwell, which is separate from the building.

Alternatively, it is possible to arrange the access to the safety stairwell via a safety lock. Using a smoke purge system with controlled pressure maintenance, that is, a smoke pressure system, positive pressure is created in the stairwell, which prevents smoke from entering. In many cases a preceding safety lock is stipulated as an anteroom, which is intended as an additional means of stopping smoke from entering the safety stairwell.

Necessary staircases without necessary stairwell Not all necessary staircases are located in a necessary stairwell. Where a necessary staircase is used in a low-rise residential building with a low fire risk or as an internal means of circulation within a two-story functional unit, this staircase does not require enclosure in a stairwell. This means that this type of open staircase can be used as an escape and rescue route.

External staircase External staircases where the rescue route is not at risk in the case of a fire due to their safe design do not require enclosure in a stairwell either. This means that such an external staircase must be located at a place alongside the external wall where there are no windows. If it can only be installed in a place where there are windows, the windows must be fitted with fire protection glazing. > Fig. 47

Fig. 47: External staircase

ADDITIONAL FORMS OF SECOND RESCUE ROUTES

Where a structural second rescue route is not stipulated, there are other means of providing this second rescue route. For example, a functional unit at ground level can have an additional door (terrace door or back door) that leads from the functional unit to the open, or the open can be reached by climbing through a window. For units in the upper floors, the second rescue route can be provided via windows or balconies provided they are suitable for the fire service's rescue equipment (e.g. ladders). > Fig. 48

Fig. 48: Examples of second rescue routes

From basements, it is also possible to provide second rescue routes via adequately sized windows that lead to walk-through light shafts or via outside staircases. If the option through a window is chosen, the sill height must be low enough and the light shaft must be large enough for people to use it. > Fig. 49

Where a habitable room exists in the loft, an adequately sized window that can be reached by a ladder can also be used as a second rescue route. However, the loft window must be close enough to the eaves so that it is possible to step over to the ladder that has been placed against the eaves. > Fig. 50 Alternatively, it is possible to install an escape window with an escape platform in front of it allowing people to get close enough to the eaves/ladder.

Should there be no habitable room in either the basement or the loft but only storage cubicles, for example, only one rescue route has to be provided.

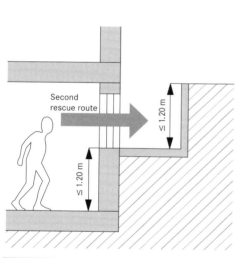

Fig. 49: Second rescue route from basement

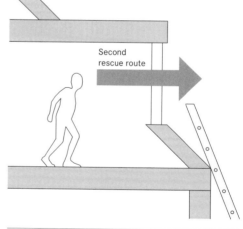

Fig. 50: Second rescue route from the loft

Organizational measures

Organizational measures may be required in addition to structural and plant-related measures of preventive fire protection.

PREVENTING FIRE

Many fires are caused by electricity and carelessness in the handling of fire, by hazardous substances, or as a result of working with a cutting or grinding disk. For this reason, caution and careful behavior are essential for preventing fires. In companies, the operatives must be instructed on the risks that are associated with activities such as welding or handling chemical substances. In addition, fuse boxes, sockets, and electric equipment must be regularly checked because they tend to overheat when defective and can thereby cause a fire. > Tab. 15

Tab. 15: Examples of passive and active fire prevention

Passive and active fire prevention
Work-related
— Do not leave open fire unattended
— Do not use water to extinguish grease fires
— Do not use flammable substances near an open fire and maintain the necessary safety distance to combustible substances
— Empty ash into lidded, non-combustible containers
— Operate and service furnaces and smoke extraction systems in accordance with regulations
— When carrying out work with a cutting or grinding disk, secure the workplace at an appropriate distance because hot particles and sparks are a considerable fire risk
— When carrying out soldering and welding work, maintain the necessary safety distance to combustible substances
— Store rags soaked in oil, petrol, or spirit in non-combustible containers
Electricity
— Only use professionally tested electrical equipment
— When using radiant heaters, lamps, and other heat-producing appliances, maintain an adequate safety distance to combustible substances
— Switch off electrical equipment after use
— Ask professionals to carry out electric installations and repairs
— When drilling or driving nails into plaster, check that there is no concealed wiring
Escape and rescue routes
— Do not obstruct escape and rescue routes and emergency exits
— Do not leave fire loads on escape and rescue routes
— Do not prevent smoke control and fire doors from closing using a wedge
— Do not place objects underneath fire and smoke control shutters or fire and smoke control curtains that would prevent these devices from closing properly

ORGANIZATIONAL AND OPERATIONAL MEASURES

Should a fire occur in a building, the users of the building must be able to detect, find, and use escape routes and self-help equipment. These items must be clearly designated to ensure that they can be seen in the case of a fire. If the building is used by many people who are not familiar with it or who are restricted in their mobility, more rescue signs must be displayed so that deviations can be avoided (safety guidance system). > Chapter Emergency power supply and lighting / rescue signs

Fire service plans As a rule, special buildings require fire service plans. These consist of a text section and floor layout plans; they help to provide the fire service with an overview of the building or parts of the building. The content of these documents is determined in cooperation with the Fire Protection Agency or the respective fire service; items to be included are those that are relevant for firefighting operations, for example, access, fire sections, fire safety installations, and areas for placing/parking equipment and vehicles. One set of the fire service plans is handed to the respective fire service and one remains in the building, for example with the porter or with the central fire alarm panel. It is important to ensure that the fire service plans are always kept up to date, for example after a conversion of the building.

Firefighting maps Buildings fitted with a fire alarm system need firefighting maps. These special maps show in what part of the building, and on what floor, the automatic alarms of the fire alarm system that were triggered can be found.

Inspections and maintenance Furthermore, it is important to ensure that the escape and rescue routes and the local extinguishing devices can be used at any time. In companies and larger units, fire protection officers have to be appointed and trained; these will ensure that extinguishing equipment is regularly serviced and checked for proper function and that rescue routes in the premises are not obstructed. In larger companies, this is checked in the form of regular controls by the fire service. > Fig. 51

The scope of these measures in special buildings is determined with the help of a risk assessment, for example at the workplace, workshop, or sports venue, taking into account the number of employees and the number of guests, customers, or visitors in the building.

O **Note:** The fire protection officer is responsible for implementing, monitoring, and adapting the organizational fire protection in a company or institution and is supported by fire protection assistants. Fire protection assistants are trained for their task in both theory and practice. This includes learning how to operate the various extinguishing devices so that, in the case of a fire, they can be deployed as first firefighters of incipient fires.

Fig. 51: Obstacles on the rescue route

Workplaces must comply with the statutory building codes and, in addition, operational measures must be carried out to guarantee the safety of operatives. Members of staff are trained in how to behave in the case of a fire. The prevention of fire and the behavior in the case of a fire are defined in a Fire Safety Policy, which is part of organizational fire protection. Part of the Fire Safety Policy is posted in a public place to enable employees and other people in the building (guests, tradespeople, customers) to obtain the necessary information about correct behavior in the case of a fire. > Fig. 52

Possible instructions for behavior in the case of a fire:

Workplaces

Behavior in the case of a fire

— Remain calm
— Use the manual fire alarm to report the fire
— Inform the relevant fire service, using the alarm template:
    — Who?
    — What?
    — How many injured?
    — What type of injury?
— Wait for questions
— Inform people in the building
— Do not use elevators
— Attempt to extinguish the fire
— Do not put your own safety at risk
— Follow further instructions
— Follow the escape and rescue route signs to the emergency exit
— Go to the assembly point
— Report the situation to the fire service

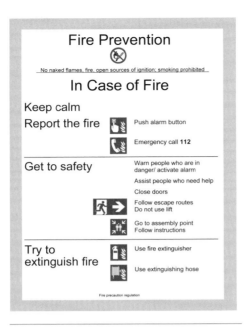

Fig. 52: Example: "Fire Prevention Regulation", Part A
as per DIN 14096

In buildings with special functions – such as hospitals, sheltered accommodation for elderly residents, and public buildings – the needs of people with restricted mobility, or those of sick people, must be taken into consideration when planning for the fire risk. This involves the training of assistants who are staff members and can help these people with their escape. Special devices are provided, such as evacuation chairs or evacuation mattresses. > Figs. 53–54

○ **Note**: In Germany, Fire Safety Policies are set out in accordance with DIN 14096 (Fire Prevention Regulations). They comprise Parts A, B, and C. Part A is an information sheet for all members of staff and visitors that is posted in a public place and contains the usual rules of behavior in the case of a fire. Part B is used to explain the use of self-help equipment in the building. This part must be made available to the employees and contains exact instructions for the prevention of fire and on how to behave in the case of a fire. Members of staff who have to carry out special tasks in the event of a fire, i.e. fire protection officers, fire protection assistants, and safety officers, obtain instructions that are defined in Part C.

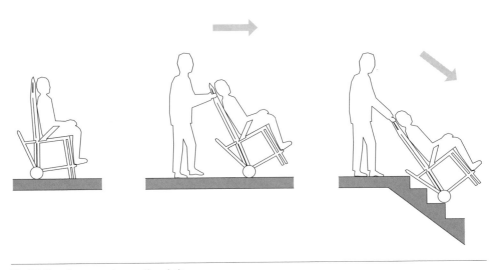

Fig. 53: Use of a rescue/evacuation chair

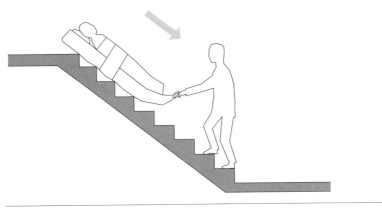

Fig. 54: Rescue/evacuation mattress

Defensive fire protection measures

When there is a fire, the fire service is called for help. This can be done via an emergency call or by triggering a fire alarm system that has a direct link to the fire service. The first task of the fire service is to rescue animals and people who cannot independently leave the danger zone. The next step is to start with the extinguishing operations and to secure the surrounding area, for example by cooling the neighboring buildings in order to prevent ignition. These active (extinguishing, rescue) and passive measures (fire prevention) are referred to as defensive fire protection.

FIRE SERVICE DUTIES

The main duties of the fire service include:
— Protecting
— Rescuing
— Extinguishing
— Retrieving

Protecting

Protecting operations include assistance in public emergencies (e.g. forest fire) through to averting risks to the environment (e.g. pollutant measurements, dealing with extinguishing agents that are hazardous to the environment, such as those containing fluoride or halogen). Furthermore, the fire service controls extinguishing facilities and provides fire safety guards during public events or performances.

Rescuing

Where people or animals are at risk, the fire service is responsible for carrying out technical rescue operations. This includes placing a portable or turntable ladder at a building in order to provide a second rescue route, and also rescue operations in other dangerous situations (rescue from a vehicle after an accident, or rescue from a high place, from floods, or after accidents related to ice).

Extinguishing

Once the fire service has completed the rescue operations, it will start with extinguishing measures. The fire will be controlled with carefully planned extinguishing measures and finally extinguished. Should there be a risk of the fire re-igniting, the fire service will provide a fireguard. A fireguard will observe what is happening and, should the fire break out again and further actions have to be initiated, will inform the fire service's command center.

Retrieving

It is not always possible to rescue all people or animals from a dangerous situation (natural disasters, fires, accidents). Those that have not survived the event are retrieved by the fire service. Finally, the fire service is responsible for securing items and evidence and for ensuring that the site where the event occurred is cleared.

The fire service defines protection objectives such as response time, scope of deployment, and degree of achievement to help with the performance of their various duties.

The time from receiving the fire alarm to the arrival of the fire service at the place of deployment is referred to as response time. The faster the fire service can carry out this first step, the greater is the chance of preventing the spread of the fire. The stipulations for response time are subject to different regulations in the different States; this is due to the different urban densities and different potential hazards. Where a short response time is required, that is, a response time of about eight minutes, a close-knit network of fire stations with appropriate staffing must be in place and available. The length of the response time also has consequences for the structural requirements, because the longer the response time is before the fire service arrives, the longer the building must be able to resist a fire, and self-rescuing must be possible.

Response time

Before a fire service team is deployed to attend a fire, the size of the team (how many units) and the firefighting equipment used by the team and taken to the place of deployment are determined for each event.

Scope of deployment

The degree of achievement is a way of checking that the response time is achieved and that the scope of deployment is appropriate. The degree of achievement is determined beforehand (e.g. 90 percent) and the idea is that this is achieved with the means provided. Owing to special weather conditions or parallel deployments, or other unforeseeable events, it is possible that this is not achieved, and that the degree of achievement drops to 75 percent. In that case, measures must be taken that improve the scope of performance of the fire service (more personnel, training, additional vehicles and equipment) in order to ensure that the defined protection objectives of the respective municipality can be fulfilled.

Degree of achievement

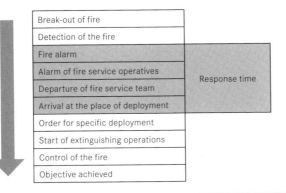

Fig. 55: Sequence of fire service operations diagram

The tasks of defensive fire protection can be carried out by different forms of fire service. This depends partly on the arrangements applicable in the different States, and partly on the size of the municipality and the potential hazards. The protection of the population is primarily the responsibility of the public fire service which, depending on size, may be organized as a professional service or a voluntary service. Larger companies that deal with hazardous goods on the company premises or require these for their production often employ an in-house company fire service team. This may be on a voluntary basis or may have been a condition imposed by the municipality or insurance company. Large chemical companies or refineries have their own in-house fire service teams to prevent damage; these teams receive special training tailored to the respective hazard and also often have special equipment or materials for firefighting. This makes it possible to significantly shorten the response time, and hence to avoid more extensive damage. In turn, this helps to minimize the downtime of production operations in the case of a fire. Large airports, too, have their own fire service. Their main task consists of fighting fires on the aviation side. For this purpose the airport fire service is equipped with special vehicles that have to stand by at every take-off and every landing. As a rule, the specified response time at airports is three minutes. > Tab. 16

Tab. 16: Different organizational forms of fire service

In-house fire service	Public fire service
Works fire service	Professional fire service
Port fire service	Voluntary fire service
Airport fire service	
Company fire service	

USING RESCUE EQUIPMENT

Accessibility

If the second rescue route to a building is to be provided via the fire service's rescue equipment, the prerequisites for this must be established at an early stage in the design to make it possible for the fire service to reach the building and to place its vehicles and equipment. This means that access to these areas must be via a public highway or, if they are too far away from such a highway, via a secured access zone. Where, in the case of a block development, access roads or pedestrian passages are planned for the fire service so that rescue and extinguishing operations can also take place at the rear of the building or from an inner courtyard, these access routes must be designed with appropriate dimensions. This means that access roads and pedestrian access passages for the rescue vehicles must be adequate in terms of height and width. Where only a pedestrian access passage through the building is to be provided, this must be designed so that fire service operatives carrying a portable ladder can go through it. This results in minimum dimensions of 1.25 m in width and 2 m in height. > Fig. 56 If it is intended that the rear of the building can be reached by aerial rescue trucks via an access drive, the respective minimum dimensions also need to be taken into account. The width of these access drives depends on the external dimensions of the rescue vehicles that will approach the building in the case of a fire. > Figs. 57–58 These dimensions vary a great deal depending on the model of fire service vehicle, and should therefore be discussed with the respective fire service. A suitable hardstanding must be available for placing the aerial rescue trucks. This means that it must be large enough to accommodate and secure the vehicle. It is also important that the hardstanding is structurally sound, especially when it is located above underground parking garages or basements.

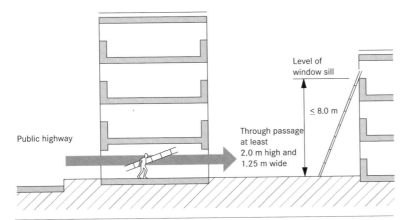

Fig. 56: Pedestrian passage for fire operative with rescue ladder

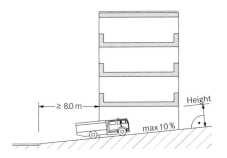

Fig. 57: Height and width of a through passage for fire service vehicles

Fig. 58: Height of through-passage where the terrain is sloping

The rescue service is only available up to a certain height (nominal rescue height). The respective ladders (portable ladders or turntable ladder) have to be placed at certain angles (about 65 to 75 degrees) for them to be leaning safely against the building and allowing rescue operations. This means that adequate space must be available on the ground next to the building so that the ladders can be placed at the required distance; where an aerial rescue truck with a turntable ladder is used, an adequate
○ hardstanding must be available. > Fig. 33

FACILITATING EXTINGUISHING WORK

Reliable supply of extinguishing water

Once rescue operations have been completed, the fire service starts extinguishing operations. To do this, the building must have a reliable supply of extinguishing water, for example via hydrants in the immediate vicinity of the building or via dry/wet (permanently filled with water) rising mains in the case of larger buildings.

> ○ **Note**: Normally it is easier to access a freestanding building because there is clear access to all external walls of the building. Furthermore, it is possible to leave the burning building on more than one side and also to fight the fire from different sides of the building. In a block development this is only possible from the street side or from the rear of the block.

Fig. 59: Pillar hydrant

Once the fire service has completed rescue operations, the operatives will attack the fire via the structural rescue route. The type and duration of extinguishing operations depend on the phase of the fire (incipient fire, developed fire, fully developed fire) and are also influenced by phenomena that occur in parallel to the fire. > Chapter Development of a fire These parallel phenomena include high temperatures, the development of smoke that reduces visibility, and toxic gases that make the use of breathing apparatus necessary. > Chapter Smoke Extinguishing operations will continue until the fire is under control and finally extinguished.

In Conclusion

The statutory regulations of fire protection in each State are extensive and vary, which means that when a project is planned the content of this book must be compared with the respective applicable regulations and standards. However, in order to be able to use these statutory instruments, budding architects must have a basic understanding of fire protection objectives, and preventive and defensive fire protection, in order to be able to use the information in their own designs.

Even at the very initial stages of the layout design, considerations relating to fire protection play an important role. Without a comprehensive overview, the designer is forced to rely on dimensions and provisions included in the standards. It is not possible to develop unique and good designs that achieve the protection objectives unless one understands how the different aspects interrelate. In professional life, the cooperation with fire protection experts involves discussions and agreement in the search for optimum solutions for a safe and – at the same time – attractive building.

Appendix

BIBLIOGRAPHY

Lutz Battran, Josef Mayr: *Handbuch Brandschutzatlas,* Rudolf Müller
Publishers, Cologne 2018

Bert Bielefeld: *Planning Architecture: Dimensions and Typologies,*
Birkhäuser, Basel 2016

Gerd Geburtig: *Baulicher Brandschutz im Bestand,* Beuth Publishers,
Berlin 2012

Sylvia Heilmann: *Brandschutz in Kindergärten, Schulen und Hoch-*
schulen, Verlag für Brandschutzpraxis, Cologne 2012

Dietmar Hosser: *Leitfaden Ingenieurmethoden des Brandschutzes,*
Ebner Publishers, Bremen 2013

Verein Deutscher Ingenieure e.V.: *VDI Guideline 3819, Brandschutz*
für Gebäude, Beuth Publishers, Düsseldorf 2016

Richard Welter, Dirk Richelmann: *The State Building Code of*
North Rhine-Westphalia in Pictures, Rudolf Müller Publishers,
Cologne 2013

Robert W. Fitzgerald, Brian J. Meacham: *Fire Performance Analysis*
for Buildings, Wiley, Hoboken 2017

Robert C. Till, J. Walter Coon: *Fire Protection – Detection, Notification,*
and Suppression, Springer, Cham 2018

National Fire Protection Association, Society of Fire Protection
Engineers: *SFPE Engineering Guide to Performance-Based Fire*
Protection, National Fire Protection Association, Quincy 2007

Society of Fire Protection Engineers: *SFPE Guide to Human Behavior*
in Fire, Springer, Cham 2018

ONLINE LITERATURE

Deutsche Gesetzliche Unfallversicherung e.V.: *Aufgaben, Qualifikation,*
Ausbildung und Bestellung von Brandschutzbeauftragten, Berlin
2014, https://publikationen.dguv.de

Gabriele Famers, Joseph Messerer: *"Rettung von Personen" und*
"wirksame Löscharbeiten" – bauordnungsrechtliche Schutzziele mit
Blick auf die Entrauchung, position paper of the Building Control
Committee, 2009, www.is-argebau.de

Home Office, Department for Communities and Local Government, *Fire*
Safety – Risk Assessment: Offices and Shops, London June 2006,
https://www.gov.uk

Institut für Schadenverhütung und Schadenforschung der öffentlichen
Versicherer e.V., *Ursachenstatistik Brandschäden 2018,* Kiel 2018,
www.ifs-ev.org

Thomas Kempen: *Materieller Brandschutz nach BauO NRW,* Bund
    Deutscher Baumeister, Architekten und Ingenieure e.V., Bezirks-
    gruppe Aachen, Aachen 2017, www.bdb-aachen.de
Ministry for Regional Identity, Communities and Local Government,
    Building and Gender Equality of the Land of North Rhine-
    Westphalia: *Handlungsempfehlung auf der Grundlage der Dienst-
    besprechungen mit den Bauaufsichtsbehörden,* Düsseldorf 2019,
    www.mhkbg.nrw
Ministry of Housing and Urban-Rural Development of the People's
    Republic of China and the General Administration of Quality
    Supervision, Inspection and Quarantine of the People's Republic of
    China, *Code for fire protection design of buildings Guo Biao 50016-
    2014,* Beijing May 2015, www.wdfxw.net
Ministry of Housing, Communities & Local Government, *Approved
    Document B,* London December 2010, www.gov.uk
Fabian Müller: *Einsatztaktik für die Feuerwehr Hinweise zur Ventilation
    bei Brandeinsätzen,* Baden-Württemberg State Fire Service School,
    Bruchsal 2016, www.lfs-bw.de
Tanja Muth et al: *Leistungsfähigkeit von Rettungsgeräten der Feuerwehr
    bei der Rettung von Personen aus Obergeschossen baulicher
    Anlagen,* Fire Protection Technology Research Unit, Karlsruhe
    2016, www.ffb.kit.edu
Jochen Stein: *Qualitätskriterien für die Bedarfsplanung von Feuerwehren
    in Städten,* Working Group of the Heads of Fire Services (AGBF
    Bund im Deutschen Städtetag), Bonn 2015, www.agbf.de
VdS Schadenverhütung GmbH: *Notwendigkeit von Brandschutz-
    beauftragten,* VdS Publishers, Cologne 2018, https://vds.de

LAWS/GUIDELINES/RULES

Administrative Provisions – Technical Building Rules (MVV TB),
    January 2017
Labor Protection Law (ArbSchG), August 1996
Law on Fire Protection, General Aid, and Disaster Control (BHKG),
    December 2015
Model Building Code (MBO), November 2002
Model High-Rise Buildings Directive (MHHR), April 2008
Model Industrial Buildings Directive (MIndBauRL), July 2017
Model Ordinance Governing Sales Premises (MVKVO), September 1995
North-Rhine Westphalia Building Code 2018 (BauO NRW 2018),
    July 2018
North-Rhine Westphalia Special Building Ordinance (SBauVO),
    December 2016
Technical Rules for Workplaces (ASR), May 2018

STANDARDS (SELECTION)

BS 9999	Fire safety in the design, management and use of buildings. Code of practice
DIN 4102	Fire behavior of building materials and elements
DIN 14096	Fire precaution regulation – Rules for drafting and placarding
DIN 18040	Construction of accessible buildings – Design principles
DIN 18232	Smoke and heat control systems
DIN EN 1365	Fire resistance tests for loadbearing elements
DIN EN 1634	Fire resistance and smoke control tests for door and shutter assemblies, openable windows
DIN EN 13501	Fire classification of construction products and building elements
DIN ISO 23601	Safety identification – Escape and evacuation plan signs

PHOTO CREDITS
Title photo by Bert Bielefeld
Fig. 21, fig. 23 by Scott Lambeth
Fig. 47 from Pixabay
All other photos by Diana Helmerking

Drawings:
Marijana Mariç
Marga-Maria Weidt

AUTHOR

Diana Helmerking, Dipl.-Ing (FH), architect, scientific staff member at the Department of Construction Economics and Construction Management at the University of Siegen, Germany

Basics Roof Construction
Tanja Brotrück
ISBN 978-3-7643-7683-3

Basics Timber Construction
Ludwig Steiger
ISBN 978-3-7643-8102-8

Basics Steel Construction
Katrin Hanses
ISBN 978-3-0356-0370-5

Available as a compendium:
Basics Building Construction
Bert Bielefeld (ed.)
ISBN 978-3-0356-0372-9

Professional Practice
Basics Budgeting
Bert Bielefeld,
Roland Schneider
ISBN 978-3-03821-532-5

Basics Project Planning
Hartmut Klein
ISBN 978-3-7643-8469-2

Basics Project Control
Pecco Becker
ISBN 978-3-0356-1666-8

Basics Site Management
Lars-Phillip Rusch
ISBN 978-3-7643-8104-2

Basics Tendering
Tim Brandt, Sebastian Franssen
ISBN 978-3-7643-8110-3

Basics Time Management
Bert Bielefeld
ISBN 978-3-7643-8873-7

Available as a compendium:
Basics Project Management
Architecture
Bert Bielefeld (ed.)
ISBN 978-3-03821-462-5

Urbanism
Basics Urban Analysis
Gerrit Schwalbach
ISBN 978-3-7643-8938-3

Basics Urban Building Blocks
Thorsten Bürklin, Michael Peterek
ISBN 978-3-7643-8460-9

**Building Services/
Building Physics**
Basics Lighting Design
Roman Skowranek
ISBN 978-3-0356-0930-1

Basics Room Conditioning
Oliver Klein, Jörg Schlenger
ISBN 978-3-7643-8664-1

Basics Water Cycles
Doris Haas-Arndt
ISBN 978-3-7643-8854-6

Available as a compendium:
Basics Building Technology
Bert Bielefeld (ed.)
ISBN 978-3-0356-0928-8

Available at your bookshop or at
www.birkhauser.com

Series editor: Bert Bielefeld

Concept: Bert Bielefeld, Annette Gref

Translation from German into English:
Hartwin Busch

English copy editing: Patricia Kot

Project management: Annette Gref

Production: Amelie Solbrig

Layout, cover design, and typography:
Andreas Hidber

Typesetting: Sven Schrape

Papier: Magno Natural, 120 g/m²
Druck: Beltz Grafische Betriebe,
Bad Langensalza

Library of Congress Control Number:
2019952677

Bibliographic information published by the
German National Library

The German National Library lists this publica-
tion in the Deutsche Nationalbibliografie; de-
tailed bibliographic data are available on the
Internet at http://dnb.dnb.de.

ISBN 978-3-0356-1859-4
e-ISBN (PDF) 978-3-0356-1936-2
e-ISBN (EPUB) 978-3-0356-1929-4
German Print-ISBN 978-3-0356-1858-7

© 2020 Birkhäuser Verlag GmbH, Basel
P.O. Box 44, 4009 Basel, Switzerland
Part of Walter de Gruyter GmbH, Berlin/Boston

9 8 7 6 5 4 3 2 1
www.birkhauser.com